W9-CCP-537

WILD! Exploring Animal Habitats

CREATURES IN A
WET
RAIN FOREST

Francine Topacio

PowerKiDS
press.

New York

Published in 2020 by The Rosen Publishing Group, Inc.
29 East 21st Street, New York, NY 10010

Editor: Elizabeth Krajnik
Book Design: Reann Nye

Photo Credits: Cover Rene Holtslag/Shutterstock.com; Series Art SaveJungle/ Shutterstock.com; p. 5 Asif Islam/Shutterstock.com; p. 7 Dmitriy Bryndin/ Shutterstock.com; p. 8 wasanajai/Shutterstock.com; p. 9 Carlos Macapuna/ Moment/Getty Images; p. 10 Tom Black Dragon/Shutterstock.com; p. 11 GUDKOV ANDREY/Shutterstock.com; p. 13 ToniFlap/iStock / Getty Images Plus/ Getty Images; p. 14 skaman306/Moment/Getty Images; p. 15 Ryan M. Bolton/ Shutterstock.com; p. 16 Ondrej Prosicky/Shutterstock.com; p. 17 PhotocechCZ/ Shutterstock.com; p. 18 Jakub Koziol/Shutterstock.com; p.19 Mark_Kostich/ Shutterstock.com; p. 21 ©Juan Carlos Vindas/Moment/Getty Images; p. 22 ProDesign studio/Shutterstock.com.

Library of Congress Cataloging-in-Publication Data

Names: Topacio, Francine, author.
Title: Creatures in a wet rain forest / Francine Topacio.
Description: Revised edition. | New York : PowerKids Press, 2020. | Series: Wild! Exploring animal habitats | Includes index.
Identifiers: LCCN 2019009983| ISBN 9781725304369 (paperback) | ISBN 9781725304383 (library bound) | ISBN 9781725304376 (6 pack)
Subjects: LCSH: Rain forest ecology–Juvenile literature. | Rain forest animals–Juvenile literature. | Habitat (Ecology)–Juvenile literature.
Classification: LCC QH541.5.R27 T67 2020 | DDC 577.34–dc23
LC record available at https://lccn.loc.gov/2019009983

Manufactured in the United States of America

CPSIA Compliance Information: Batch #CSPK19. For Further Information contact Rosen Publishing, New York, New York at 1-800-237-9932.

CONTENTS

RAIN FOREST BASICS

Rain forests are forests found in places where it rains a lot—usually more than 70 inches (177.8 cm) each year—and is usually warm and **humid**. The trees found in rain forests are evergreen. Tropical rain forests are found in South and Central America, West and Central Africa, Indonesia, parts of Southeast Asia, and tropical Australia.

"Dry rain forests" are rain forests in places that have a dry season, such as northeastern Australia. There, it only rains between 31.5 and 70.8 inches (80 and 180 cm) a year. This book focuses on tropical rain forests.

Temperate rain forests, like the one pictured here in Olympic National Park in Washington State, receive between 60 and 200 inches (152 and 508 cm) of rain each year.

5

RAIN FOREST LAYERS

Tropical rain forests are divided into four **layers**. The lowest layer is the forest floor. The forest floor is very dark, hot, and moist. Few plants grow there. Animals big and small live on the forest floor.

The understory is home to plants such as small trees and large-leafed bushes. Many animals and insects live in the understory.

The canopy is made up of the tops of trees. Lots of sunlight and rain reach this layer. Birds, monkeys, snakes, and other animals live in the canopy.

The emergent layer is made up of the tallest trees. Many animals, such as eagles, monkeys, bats, and butterflies live in the emergent layer.

Creature Corner

Even though tropical rain forests cover only about 6 percent of Earth's land, about one-half to three-quarters of Earth's plant and animal species, or kinds, live there.

Plants in tropical rain forests lose water through holes in their leaves very quickly. This moisture feeds clouds, which hold rain. This process happens very fast because of how hot it is. This is why rain forests are so rainy and steamy!

GIANT GREENHOUSES

Tropical rain forests are like greenhouses because they're warm and humid. This is the perfect **environment** for plants to grow in. Tropical rain forests are home to more than two-thirds of the world's plant species. These plants are food and cover for many rain forest animals. Bees and butterflies depend on the pollen from colorful flowers for food. Monkeys snack on the trees' fruits and leaves.

Creature Corner

People use the fibers from the kapok tree's seedpods for many things, including stuffing pillows. Birds also make their nests in the kapok tree's branches.

The most common tree species in the Amazon rain forest is *Euterpe precatoria*, which is a type of palm tree **related** to the açaí palm. People and animals eat the berries from these trees.

Tropical rain forests are sometimes called Earth's lungs. This is because rain forest plants take in a harmful gas called carbon dioxide and turn it into a gas called oxygen, which all animals need to live.

THE FOREST FLOOR

The forest floor is home to many rain forest animals. Animals here are herbivores, or animals that only eat plants; carnivores, or animals that only eat meat; and omnivores, or animals that eat both plants and meat.

Creature Corner

Army ants travel in huge **swarms** of more than 300,000 ants! They eat any insect or small animal that can't get out of the swarm's path.

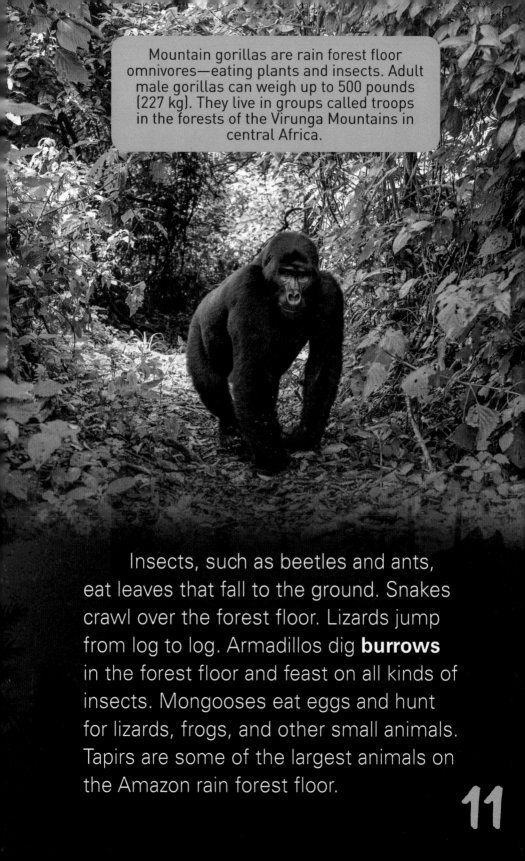

Mountain gorillas are rain forest floor omnivores—eating plants and insects. Adult male gorillas can weigh up to 500 pounds (227 kg). They live in groups called troops in the forests of the Virunga Mountains in central Africa.

Insects, such as beetles and ants, eat leaves that fall to the ground. Snakes crawl over the forest floor. Lizards jump from log to log. Armadillos dig **burrows** in the forest floor and feast on all kinds of insects. Mongooses eat eggs and hunt for lizards, frogs, and other small animals. Tapirs are some of the largest animals on the Amazon rain forest floor.

THE GREEN ANACONDA

Green anacondas are the biggest snakes in the world. They're members of the boa family and live in wet areas on land and slow-moving streams in the tropical rain forests of the Amazon and Orinoco **basins**.

Green anacondas eat large animals including wild pigs, turtles, birds, deer, caimans, capybaras, and even jaguars. They wait in the water with just their eyes and nose showing. Then, they attack. Green anacondas kill their **prey** by wrapping their strong bodies around the prey and squeezing the animal until it can't breathe anymore. Then, they swallow their prey whole. Green anacondas can go weeks or months without food depending on the size of their prey.

Creature Corner

The longest green anaconda ever seen was more than 37 feet (11 m) long! That's about as long as a school bus.

Other kinds of anaconda, such as the yellow anaconda, also live in South America. However, these anacondas are smaller than the green anaconda.

GREEN ANACONDA

THE UNDERSTORY

Animal life in the understory is very special. Many insects use **camouflage** to stay safe from predators. Some look like sticks or leaves, trick predators into thinking they're poisonous, or look like bird poop. Understory **reptiles** also use camouflage to stay safe. Some are colored to blend in with the plant life. Camouflage also helps predators catch their prey.

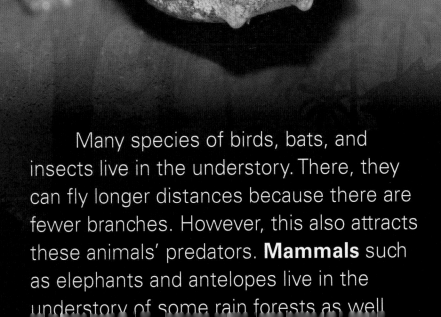

This rare Amazon climbing salamander lives in the understory of the Peruvian Amazon rain forest. Amphibians need humid air to keep their skin moist. If they dry out, they'll die.

Many species of birds, bats, and insects live in the understory. There, they can fly longer distances because there are fewer branches. However, this also attracts these animals' predators. **Mammals** such as elephants and antelopes live in the understory of some rain forests as well

BIG CATS OF THE RAIN FOREST

Many species of big cats, including jaguars, tigers, and leopards, call rain forests around the world home. Jaguars are the largest big cat species in South America. Jaguars hunt and eat wild pigs, deer, fish, and almost anything else they can find. They wait for their prey in the trees, on the ground, or in the water. Then, they ambush, or surprise attack, their prey, killing it with one bite.

Jaguars look similar to leopards. You can tell them apart because jaguars' rosettes, which are the black circles on their fur, have a spot inside them. Leopards' rosettes don't have a spot inside them.

Jaguars appeared in the **mythology** of the Maya people of South America. They thought jaguars were beautiful and powerful. People have hunted jaguars for their beautiful fur for many years. This is one reason why there aren't many jaguars left in the wild today.

THE CANOPY AND EMERGENT LAYERS

The rain forest canopy forms a sort of umbrella over the understory and forest floor layers. This keeps most sunlight and rainfall from reaching the bottom two layers of the rain forest. All this sunlight and rain makes the canopy and emergent layers full of life.

Creature Corner

The smallest rain forest monkey is the pygmy marmoset. It's so small it could easily fit in your hand. They eat mostly tree sap, but they also eat bugs, nectar, and fruit.

Macaws make their nests in holes in trees of the canopy and emergent layers of the rain forest. They can be found in the rain forests of Central and South America.

Many animals living in these layers use calls to talk to each other. This is because it's hard to see more than a few feet away due to all the leaves and branches. To get around, animals living in the canopy and emergent layers fly, jump, and glide from one spot to the next.

SLOW AND STEADY

Sloths are tree-**dwelling** mammals found in the rain forests of Central and South America. Six species of sloths are separated into two families: two-toed sloths and three-toed sloths. This name is tricky, though, because all sloths have three toes on each hind foot.

These slow-moving creatures spend most of their lives hanging upside down by their strong hook-shaped claws in the rain forest canopy. However, on the ground, sloths must crawl. Sloths are surprisingly good swimmers, though!

It takes a long time for sloths' bodies to break down their food. Because of this, they eat very little! Sloths eat fruit, leaves, young flowers, and twigs.

Sloths sometimes look green because they have **algae** that grow in their fur. The algae grow because sloths move so slowly.

21

PROTECTING THE RAIN FOREST

Rain forests are home to thousands of very important plant and animal species. However, these plants and animals are helpless against human activities. Scientists say that about 80,000 acres (32,375 ha) of tropical rain forest are cut down every day, and about another 80,000 acres (32,375 ha) are being hurt every day. Some scientists also say that we lose about 50,000 plant and animal species a year.

Humans need to cut down trees to make paper, to build houses and cities, and to make room for farmland. They also take plants from rain forests for medicine. These activities can pollute and destroy rain forest animals' homes. We must work hard to protect these important places.

GLOSSARY

alga: Plantlike living things that are mostly found in water. The plural form is algae.

basin: The land drained by a river and its branches.

burrow: A hole an animal digs in the ground for shelter.

camouflage: Colors or shapes on animals that allow them to blend in with their surroundings.

dwell: To live in a place.

environment: The conditions that surround a living thing and affect the way it lives.

humid: Having a lot of moisture in the air.

layer: One part of something lying over or under another.

mammal: Any warm-blooded animal whose babies drink milk and whose body is covered with hair or fur.

mythology: Ideas that are believed by many people but that aren't true.

prey: An animal hunted by other animals for food.

related: Belonging to the same group or family because of shared qualities.

reptile: A cold-blooded animal with thin, dry pieces of skin called scales.

swarm: A large group of insects or other animals, usually in motion.

INDEX

WEBSITES

Due to the changing nature of Internet links, PowerKids Press has
developed an online list of websites related to the subject of this
book. This site is updated regularly. Please use this link to access
the list: www.powerkidslinks.com/wild/rainforest